What's This?

By Paul Shipton

Illustrated by Steve Cox

Story with pictures and key words

OXFORD

UNIVERSITY PRESS

red

square

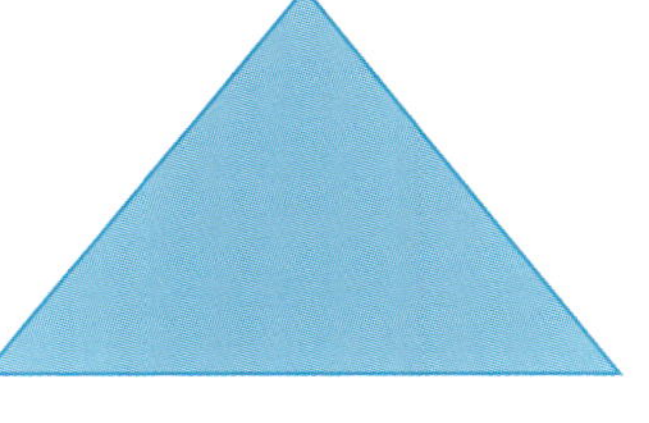

triangle

house

yellow

circle

sun

3

three

white

cloud

brown

pink

ice cream

Activity for pages 2–11

Match.

red

yellow

white

pink

ice cream

house

cloud

sun

What's This?

Story with pictures and key words

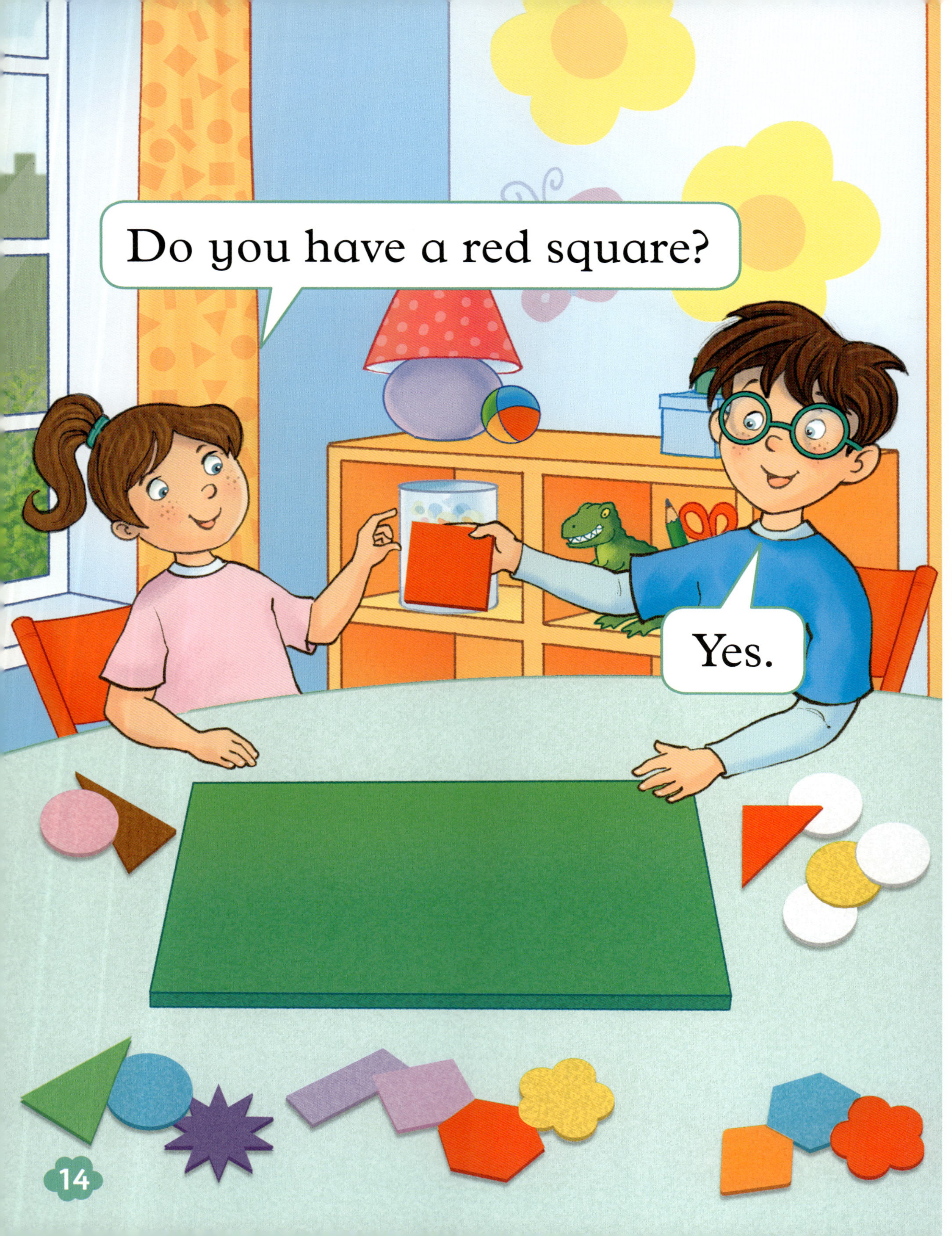

Do you have a red square?
Yes.

Do you have a red triangle?
Yes.

What's this?
It's a house.

Do you have a yellow circle?
Yes.

What's this?
It's the sun.

Do you have three white circles?
Yes.

What's this?
It's a cloud.

Do you have a brown triangle?
Yes.
21

Do you have a pink circle?
Yes.
22

What's this?
It's an ice cream!

Match.

square

circle

triangle

ice cream

house

cloud

sun